SOLDIER JOKER

CERRO GORDO OF THE MEXICAN WAR

ISBN: 978-1-257-79745-5

Publisher: LuLu.com

Rights owner: Richard Paskowitz

Copyright: 2011 Standard Copyright License

Language: English

Country: United States of America

SOLDIER JOKER

CERRO GORDO OF THE MEXICAN WAR


This is a transcription of a letter written by George Horatio Derby to his mother after the battle of Cerro Gordo.

Two officers scouted behind Santa Anna's lines. The other was Captain Robert E. Lee. Douglas Freeman's biography of Lee concerning the Battle of Cerro Gordo follows the Derby letter.

# INTRODUCTION

Prelude to Division:

The War before the War that divided US

Before the Civil War, there was  another War---the U.S. Mexican War.  This war was the result of the belief in Manifest Destiny.  That Manifest Destiny was promoted by James Polk.  It resulted in making the United States a continental country.  The side effect of the continental connection was that the country was torn asunder by diverse ideologies and beliefs, that smolder to the present day.

The  key to the battle that won the war, that determined the treaty, that won the continent, that defined the borders---was delineated in one letter. This letter contains the map of the reconnaissance plan that secured the victory of the United States over Mexico.  The letter refers to a battle plan so that Winfield Scott knew more about Santa Anna's positions than did Santa Anna.

The reconnaissance was the signature event that made possible the career of Robert E lee.  This battle, among others, secured the position of Winfield Scott to be the premier general of the United States.

Many books have been written about this war.  Causes and results are being debated to this day.  They will not be addressed here.  Suffice it to say California is now part of the United States and the Rio Grande borders the U.S. and Mexico.

Much has been written about the battle of Gettysburg and Pickett's charge.  Should we not have more discussion about the log that separated Robert E Lee from the Mexican forces.  What if he had been killed or maimed?  How would history have been changed?  And, what if George Horatio Derby would not have been wounded, and effectively removed from the Mexican war?  Consider the brilliance of teaming Robert Edward lee with George Horatio Derby?  The breast work expertise of RE Lee with the tactical and strategic, out of the box, thinking of GH Derby?

One letter, sequestered and obscured in the archives of the Military Academy At West Point.  One sentence, written just days after the battle of Cerro Gordo:" This is a little plan which I made before the attack of the positions" was written by Lieutenant Derby.  The sentence, as in the other parts of the letter, contained none of the humor and wit that would be evident in later writing by Derby under his pseudonym of John Phoenix (The Father of American Wit).  Clear, clean prose and descriptions---in the midst of battle.  The Soldier in Derby was purely manifest.  The Joker would be put on hold until later.


Forgotten by Winfield Scott were the antics of Derby while at West Point.  Remembered by General Scott was the principle of securing the best talent around him---even listening to his most junior officers--Derby--being less than one year post graduation and Robert E Lee, an army Captain at the time.


The war would be won and the players who had their first exposure to combat would go on to be major combatants in the ensuing war.  All but Derby, who would die at the age 38 in May of 1861.  He would be buried less than 100 feet from the grave of Winfield Scott.

So, in summary, we have the forgotten letter written by the forgotten man, just after the forgotten battle, that won the forgettable war, that resulted in the continental U.S., That was the prelude to the Civil War.

Enjoy, and Learn,

Memorial Day 2011

Richard A. Paskowitz, M.D.

Plan Del Rey, Mexico

April 25, 1847

My dearest Mother:

My last was written to you just after the capitulation of Veracruz and I shall take up my story from that point.

I don't know whether you will have received the letter Hardcastle was so kind as to write for me on the 20th before this, or not, probably however about the same time.  This is the eighth day from the time that I received my wound and I am now doing famously sitting up in bed writing on my knee, and suffering  no pain at all.  The Dr. is very attentive and kind and has treated me with a great deal of skill, he is just finished dressing my wound and says that in two weeks I shall be able to leave for the United States, so you may expect to see me not long after the receipt of this.

The nature of the wound is not dangerous at all. It struck on my left hip, turned on the bone, and went round my thigh.  The ball still remains in and Dr. Cuyler says it would be useless and dangerous to attempt to remove it.

We marched from Veracruz on the 11th, General Twiggs having left with his division three days previously.  On the third day of the march we were met by a courier from general Twiggs stating that the enemy were in force at Plan Del Rio and that they have fortified their position.  Knowing this pass(that of Sierra Guarda) to be the most dangerous on the road from Veracruz to Mexico City, and having but 2500 men with him, the enemy having 17,000 he had halted and waited for our coming up.  He also reported Captain Johnston of our corps as having been dangerously wounded while reconnoitering---General Scott at once made a forced march from Puente Del Rey and we arrived at this place on the 15th.  On the 16th I was ordered to reconnoiter the enemy's position which I did on both sides, passing 4 1/2 miles down his right and seeing all his lines in reverse---I made out from 12 to 15,000 Mexicans, they had a line of works throne across the road, occupied by 1800 men and mounting 12 pieces of light caliber.  The road all along from this is lined by precipitous heights which were also occupied to the extent of 4 miles.  Here there were an enormously high conical hill, called Sierra  Guarda overlooking the whole of their works and occupied by 3000 men, it was fortified and had eight pieces of artillery.

On the 17th at daylight I received orders for Major Turnbull to join general Twiggs brigade, and I reported immediately, armed, mounted, and with three days provisions.

This division was ordered to proceed to the enemies left, to open a road if possible to his rear and endeavour to get behind the Sierra Guarda.  We started at 8:00, and opening a road through the woods, we arrived about 11:00 at a point only 1/4 mile from Sierra Guarda, but concealed from it by two steep hills, covered with wood.  Here I was in front of the division, in command of a party of pioneers opening the road. Suddenly we were surprised by a rapid fire from the first hill, which from a slight sprinkle soon became a perfect hailstorm.

The brigade under the brave Colonel Harney was immediately ordered to charge and it did charge, and being attached to it myself, I charged with it.  About halfway up, my horse was shot and fell under me with a ball through his hind leg and I had to tie him up to a tree and foot it up the rest of the way, which was far preferable as the hill was so steep it was almost impossible to ride.  We drove the Mexicans from the first to the second hill, racing after them hollering and yelling like wild Indians, which last scared them as much as the firing.  They made a stand here, but we soon drove  them down with a loss of 60 killed and 140 wounded.  We lost about 30 killed and wounded.  I shot one fellow with a pistol who was about firing.  He fell and begged for his life.  I told him to lay still and nobody would touch him and went on.  But when I came back after the fight to help him I found somebody had killed him.  He was some sort of an officer and I took a sword and have got it some where now.


I believe, Lieutenant Maury, who lies now in the next bed to mine was shot through the arm on this day while gallantly leading his men up the second hill.

We occupied this hill that night and lay on our blankets.  The Mexican firing grapeshot and canister over us occasionally but with little effect.  Meanwhile by great exertion the ordnance had got two 12 pieces and a 24 to the top of the hill(which was only 300 yards from Sierra Guarda) and at sunrise we opened on them for 2 hours.  They returned our fire with interest, blazing away  from eight heavy pieces and creating horrible, havoc, Capitan Mason here lost his leg, Lieutenant Davis was killed.  Ewell, Patten, Jarvis, Dana and others were severely wounded and all was confusion.  Then Colonel Harney gave the order to charge and rushed forward himself with lieutenant Van Dorn Oakes and myself by his side.  With a wild hurra the third and seventh infantry supported by the rifles rushed over the hill.

Down we went through the whistling balls and crashing grape, men, dropping here and there, the wounded groaning, but nobody scared, and with a tremendous yell we gained the ravine and commenced the ascent of Sierra Guarda.

A fire, close, heavily and continued from 1800 muskets was opened on us, but the ascent was as extremely precipitous that it afforded us protection, for most of the balls passed over our heads.  The whistling was terrific, the air seemed alive with balls, but we went on cheering and returning the fire now and then, when we stopped for an instant to rest.  At last we came to the highest crest within 10 rods of their first breast work.  We gave  one fire, then Colonel Harney shouted with the a voice like a trumpet: " Forward boys, Forward remembered the dead!  And give it to 'em." Away we went.

The Mexicans saw us coming.  Nothing could withstand such a charge, they gave one fire and ran.  We followed, clambered up over the breast work, chased them from the tower, over the hill, turn their own pieces on them, and Sierra Guarda was ours.  Up went American flag and down came the Mexican.

It was at this moment that a retreating party going down turned and fired.  I had discharged both pistols and was standing on a little knoll directing a cannon at this same party, when I felt myself struck---I fell in the arms of a kind  fellow, named Buttrick of the rifle regiment who has been with me night and day ever since.  The victory was complete seeing us in their rear the whole army surrendered and Santa Ana ran away.

We took 5 generals, 30 colonels, 5000 men, 30 pieces of artillery and thus ended the greatest fight of the age, probably.

I had my wound dressed and at 5:00 was brought down to this place in a litter.

While lying faint from loss of blood on Sierra Guarda, General Scott came up and took me warmly by both hands.  " My poor boy  " said he," have they hit you too.  "----Colonel Harney told him the circumstances and after staying with me five or 10 minutes he left saying: "Mr. Derby, I'm proud of you sir." I felt considerably improved I assure you.

The next morning the general came over to see me and told me he had mentioned us with distinction in dispatch.  So I suppose I'll be a first lieutenant or something or other.

The army has gone to  Talapa and we are going to be moved tomorrow, so I must leave off and try to get a little rest.  I shall leave for home as soon as I can bear the journey----meanwhile rest happy and satisfied that I am doing well and have done my duty---I need not caution you not to allow this letter to me made public, it is considered highly disgraceful for an army officer to write letters to be made  public.  We leave that to volunteers.


Don't show it to anybody.  I have written in my little notebook and pull out the leaves because it is easier.  Goodbye dearest Mother.  Give my best love to dear grandmother and aunts and all enquiring friends, all of whom I hope to see in the course of two months, and believe me ever as ever,


Your affectionate son,

George H Derby

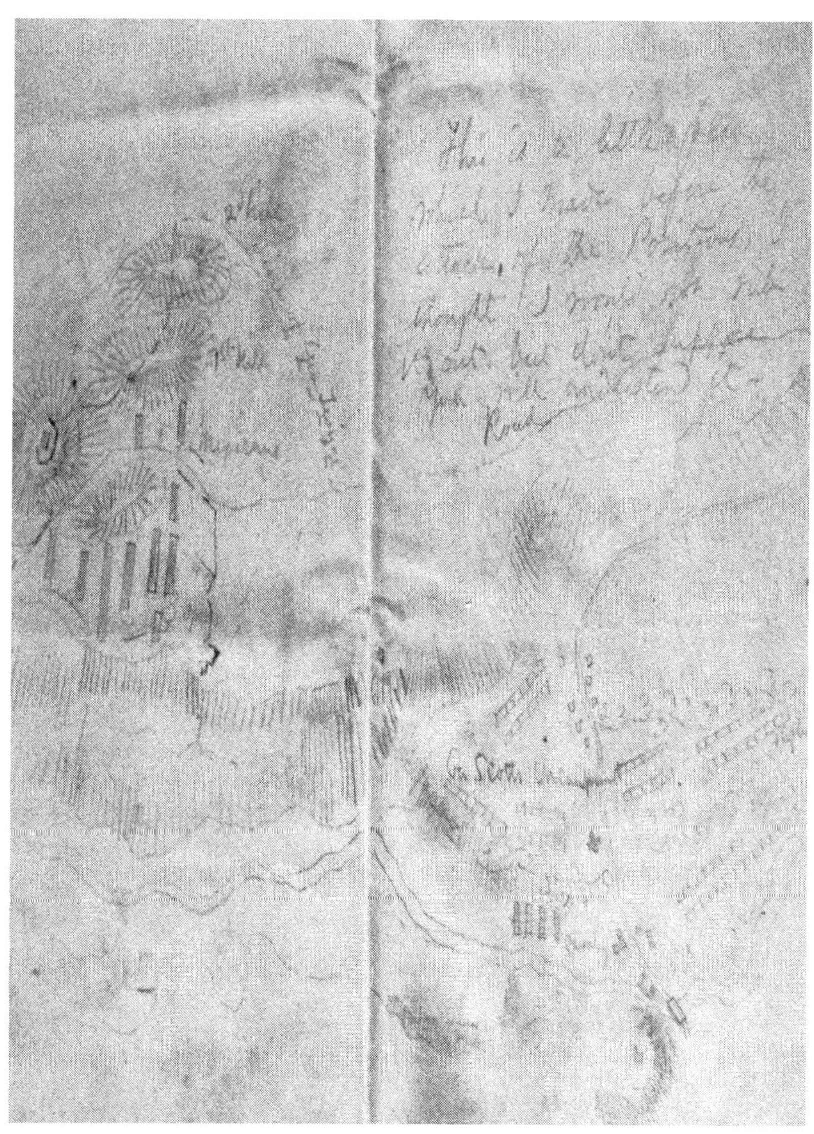

MAP OF CERRO GORDO AS DRAWN BY DERBY
IN LETTER TO MOTHER AFTER BATTLE

"This is a little plan which I made before the attack of
the positions. I thought I would not rub it out, but don't
suppose you will understand it." George Horatio Derby

BATTLE
OF
CERRO GORDO.
N.R.
A. American army
B. Battery, (American.)
C. Cerro Gordo & Tower
D. Twiggs' march.
a, a, &c. Mexican batteries.
b, b. Pillow's brigade
N. R. National road.
d. Gen. Shields' brigade.
G. Hill stormed by 2d inf.
F. 8 in. howitzer, (Amer.)

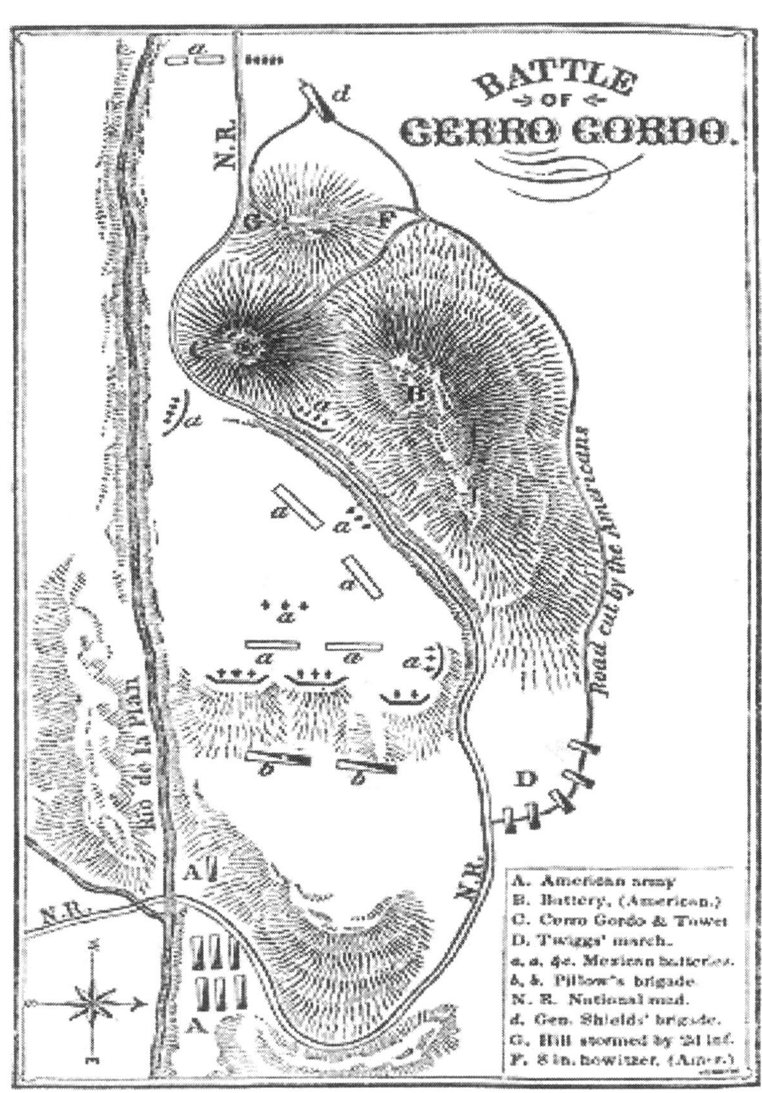

18

<u>**R. E. Lee: A Biography**</u>
<u>**by Douglas Southall Freeman**</u>
published by Charles Scribner's Sons,
New York and London, 1934

## A Day Under a Log Contributes to Victory

## (CERRO GORDO)

Less than a week after General Scott's embarrassing experience at church, Lee saw Twigg's division of regulars set out from Vera Cruz for the interior. Scott had planned from the first to find and to defeat the main army of the enemy, even if he had to march to Mexico City, and he had tarried at the coast solely because of the slow arrival of transportation. No certain news was available at the time concerning the strength, the movements, or the position of the enemy, though it was reported that General Santa Anna had hurried southward after his defeat at Buena Vista and had organized a new army with which to dispute the advance of the Americans towards his capital. To give Twiggs support in case these rumors proved true, other units of the army marched inland from day to day until April 12, when General Scott himself left Vera Cruz, accompanied by Lee and the rest of his staff. The division of Worth and a few detachments remained behind, but were to join the main army as soon as practicable. There still was no definite information of the enemy, but rumor had it that Santa Anna was already at Jalapa, •sixty miles northwest of Vera Cruz.

Anticipating the advance, Lee took advantage of the final visit to bid farewell to his brother with the fleet. He had spent one night aboard the *Mississippi*, where the visit had not been altogether a success. "He was very well," Lee wrote of Smith, "but what a place a ship is to enjoy the company of one's brother."[1]

Without more ado he joined his commander. Travelling through rich plains, which delighted the heart of Lee, the cavalcade came on April 14 to the broad and swift, though shallow, Rio del Plan at a bridge leading to a village and a pleasant p238 meadow styled Plan del Rio. The village was deserted, but the surrounding fields were covered with bowers set up by the advance American column.[2] All the troops that had preceded Scott were there, with Major General Robert Patterson in command. The men received their general in chief with loud cheers; but much as he loved it, he had little time for their applause. His subordinates had grave news for him. The enemy had been located: in a grim mountain pass that rose above Rio del Plan, Santa Anna himself, with a force estimated at 12,000 or more, was awaiting the Americans. All the extensive mountain ridges commanding the passes were held by strong Mexican batteries. General Twiggs had wished to attack on the 13th, and had planned to do so on the 14th, but had been held back by General Patterson, who did not want an action opened against a position of such strength until Scott himself was on the ground with all his forces.

Scott at once ordered a full reconnaissance. Young engineers had been working on the right of the road that led through the pass, and they had some reason to believe that a practicable route for the army might be found there.<u>3</u> Lee was directed to press the reconnaissance and to ascertain whether the enemy's position could be turned. Going out on the morning of 15th with his guide, John FitFitzwalterter, Lee found that Santa Anna had chosen his ground well. The right of the Mexicans overlooked the river, on bluffs so nearly perpendicular that it was manifestly futile to attempt a turning movement there. Back from the river the ground rose fast to three ridges that ran eastward and northeastward toward the position of the United States army. These ridges were crowned with well-sighted batteries. Just north of the ridge farthest from the river the so-called "National Road" mounted to the pass. On this thoroughfare, at a high point dominating it for •nearly a mile, was still another battery. North of the road and northwest of the ridges rose a conical hill, known as Cerro Gordo. Guns had been placed here and a tower had been erected. North and west of Cerro Gordo the strength and position of the enemy, among the high hills and deep ravines that cut the landscape, p239 were not discoverable by the Americans. Even the course of the road from Cerro Gordo northwestward toward Jalapa had not been ascertained. Roughly sketched, the terrain was assumed to be about this:<u>4</u>


Manifestly, it was as foolish to deliver the main attack up the National Road as it was to undertake a turning movement along the river. The army's only hope lay in finding a practicable way through the ravines on the

Mexican left that had been partially explored. Lee himself stated his problem thus: "The right of the Mexican line rested on the river at a perpendicular rock, unscalable by man or beast, and their left on impassable ravines; the main road was defended by field works containing thirty-five cannon; in their rear was the mountain of Cerro Gordo, surrounded by intrenchments in which were cannon and crowned by a tower overlooking all — it was around this army that it was intended to lead our troops."5

Slowly Lee worked his way up the ravines north of the river, on the Mexican left. The ground was very difficult, but to Lee it did not seem altogether impossible to construct a road over which troops might advance with proper caution. At last Lee stopped his stealthy movements to look about him. Near at hand was a spring, to which a path led from the south. This path must have been well-trampled, and the bushes around it must have been broken, for Lee at once concluded that he was in rear of the Mexican left flank. As he waited and studied the ground he heard voices and conversation in Spanish. Pausing only a moment he got a glimpse of a group of Mexican soldiers coming toward the spring. What should he do? How could he escape? There was only an instant for reflection, then silently he p240 dropped down behind a great log close to the water. Fortunately, the undergrowth was so thick by the side of the log that it formed a screen.

Louder the voices; louder, too, the sound of men making their way along the path. Soon the soldiers halted at the spring, drank deeply and paused in the shade to talk of the Yankees that were gathering under the ridge. If one of those Mexicans should chance to see the print of an American boot in the soft earth and should grow inquisitive, then it would be a quick death for Captain Lee and for Fitzwater who was hidden nearby. There would be surprise at headquarters because of Lee's non-return, and, to end all, there would be weeping at Arlington when the news came that he had gone off on reconnaissance and had never been heard of again.

Quietly Lee lay under the log, not daring to move a muscle. Soon more soldiers arrived and some of those who had first come to the spring straggled back. Was it to be so all day? Was the spring the water supply for that wing of the army? If so, then there could be no hope of escaping detection. Some one surely would begin to poke about among the bushes. Down on the log sat a Mexican; down sat another. Their backs were not three feet from Lee. At last they got up and lazily went their way. But others came and still others and began to prowl around as they chattered one to another.

There was a momentary shadow and a Mexican stepped over the log — almost on Lee. Had he slipped he would have landed squarely on the flank of the engineer. There was no prospect that all of them would go away. Lee could only pray that they would not see him.

The shadows slipped and the drowsy afternoon came. Rigid and silent, scarcely daring to breathe, Lee hugged the damp bark of the fallen tree and let the insects crawl and bite unhindered. Hours passed, hours that seemed ages, while that endless procession of thirsty soldiers came and drank and loafed. At last the air grew cooler, the shade began to blur. It was twilight. The Mexicans were less numerous. Finally they ceased to come and the last loiterer shuffled off. Silence then and tropical blackness. Not another sound on the path, only the distant buzz of voices p241 around far-off camp fires. Slowly Lee lifted his stiff joints from his refuge and slipped out. He was safe! Satan himself could not have seen in that blackness.

And now to find the way down that treacherous ravine back to the American lines. Well it was that Lee as a boy had prowled about King George's Meadows around quiet old Alexandria and had developed his sense of direction. Running now into a tree, slipping here down the side of the ravine, peering at every little watercourse to see which way it flowed and feeling at every step to discover the nature of the ground, he at last reached headquarters.6 He reported his findings, but he was by no means satisfied with them. Major Smith had also been out that day and had reached the same conclusion as Lee, but he, too, was still in some doubt whether the army could manoeuvre around the Mexican left.7 Scott directed them to continue the reconnaissance the next day and he placed at Lee's disposal a working party with which to cut a trail.8 Lee accordingly went out on the 16th and before nightfall had pushed his reconnaissance much farther. He did not reach the Jalapa road, which the Americans must occupy if they were to cut off the Mexican retreat, but he was reasonably sure that he was close to it.9 The new trail up the ravine was passable by the close of day, thanks to the efforts of the pioneer troops.

A decision had now to be reached: Either the army must remain in the valley, exposed to yellow-fever, which was expected to appear very soon, or else Scott had to attack at once; and if he attempted to drive the Mexicans from their perches he must deliver his main assault around the enemy's left flank, in the direction of Lee's and Smith's reconnaissance. There was no alternative. True, the route on the Mexican left was exposed at one point to the fire of the enemy; true, also, the distance to the Jalapa road, from the farthest point that Lee had reached, might be an upsetting factor. But Lee believed the Jalapa road was close to Cerro Gordo, and Scott thought the risks were justified. When Lee and the other engineers had reported, Scott decided to send Twiggs's division around Santa Anna's flank the next day, April p242 17, with Lee as guide. The battle was not to be opened until the second day following, April 18, as Scott desired to have the aid of Worth, who was nearing Plan del Rio with some 1600 men and a part of the siege train.10

As reveille was sounded for Twiggs's division, at 4:30 on the morning of April 17, there opened for Lee two days of the heaviest responsibility he had ever known. He left before Scott's order for the battle had been issued,11 but he doubtless knew all that was contemplated. General Gideon Pillow was to make a demonstration on the 18th, along the left of the American line, opposite the three batteries on the ridges, though it was not considered likely that his volunteers could storm such formidable positions.12 The troops in the centre, along the National Road, would have to wait until the flanking movement had forced the enemy from the commanding batteries; everything depended on

Twiggs's division, which depended on Lee. If he led the troops into a slaughter pen in the mountains, the blame would be wholly his. The mission of Twiggs's division was explicit: that afternoon (April 17) it was to occupy the approaches to Cerro Gordo, particularly the hill Atalaya, which was somewhat lower than Cerro Gordo and lay •about one-third of a mile northeast of it. This having been done, Twiggs's soldiers were to storm Cerro Gordo the next morning and were to press on until they blocked the Jalapa road. The other troops would then complete the envelopment of the Mexican forces.

With the greatest vigilance, Lee carried the men up the ravines that led around Santa Anna's left. "We . . . moved very slowly," one participant recorded, "every now and then halting half an hour or so, while the [Rifle Regiment], as skirmishers, cautiously felt the way through the chapparal° in advance."13 Lee was with the van; General Twiggs was close by. As the column approached the Mexican position absolute silence was enjoined on the men. Suddenly there was a thud and a rattle. Men stiffened themselves to the alert, only to discover that the commotion had been caused by a soldier who had slipped on a loose stone and, in trying to recover his balance, had struck his musket against his canteen. p243 Instantly the man's captain was upon him, sword in hand: "You infernal scoundrel," he roared at the top of his lungs, "I'll run you through if you don't make less noise." The spectacle of the captain brandishing his blade and the poor example of silence that he gave his company set the column laughing. The tension of the toiling line was eased, and the advance continued.

About 11 o'clock, when the column was •within 700 yards of the enemy, a company of the Seventh Infantry was sent up a hill separated by a ravine from the higher hill of Atalaya, in order to observe the movements of the Mexicans, prior to an attack against Atalaya itself. The infantrymen soon found that a Mexican force from the direction of Atalaya was advancing against them in greatly superior numbers. A clash followed in a few minutes, and as it was apparent that his movement was now discovered, Twiggs ordered two regiments forward to support the men of the Seventh Infantry and then to advance on Atalaya. Word was passed quickly. The excited soldiers formed line of battle. Just before the command was given them to go forward, one of the captains approached General Twiggs.

"I beg pardon, General," he said, "how far shall we charge them?"

"Charge them to hell," Twiggs stoutly replied.14

The First Artillery and the Rifle Regiment sprang up the hillside, quickly relieved the men of the Seventh Infantry, swept the Mexicans down the nearer hill, up Atalaya, over its crest, through a ravine — and had started up the sides of Cerro Gordo in hot pursuit before they heeded the recall. Then some of them found they could not return to their lines under the fire the Mexicans were pouring into the side of Atalaya from Cerro Gordo. There was danger, for the time being, that the vanguard would be taken prisoner by a Mexican counterattack, but this was prevented by the fire of some light guns, hurriedly pulled to the top of Atalaya.

After nightfall the venturesome vanguard returned to Atalaya, and such of the men as were not designated for special duty threw themselves on the ground and went to sleep. There was no rest for Lee, however. He felt that thus far all had gone flawlessly. p244 The troops were in an advantageous position with only a few casualties. But as the attack on Cerro Gordo the next morning promised to be a more serious affair, Lee had two special duties to perform, first to locate a battery on Atalaya, and then to see that the heavy guns which were being painfully brought forward were in position and ready to open at sunrise. Fortunately, three volunteer regiments of Shields's brigade had arrived on Twiggs's line at about 5 o'clock, and as these troops were much fresher than the regulars, they were at once put to work, under Lee's direction, hauling the heavy pieces up the hill and putting them in place. Before daylight on the 18th all was ready.15

Twiggs had consulted Lee freely on the 17th and had taken his advice with assurance. He doubtless sought Lee's counsel that night on the assignment of troops for the bloody task of the morrow. At Scott's suggestion it was decided that a part of the division was to assault Cerro Gordo as soon as the artillery opened. Simultaneously, Lee was to conduct the men of another brigade around the northern flank of Cerro Gordo and was to lead them to the supposed location of the Jalapa road, so that they could cut off the enemy's retreat, as provided in the general plan of action. Shields's brigade was to follow on this route with the same objective.

Early in the morning of the 18th Lee set out with Colonel Bennett Riley, commander of the Second

Brigade, who was to be in charge of the turning movement. About the same time fire was opened by the three guns Lee had placed on the summit of Atalaya, and the direct assault on Cerro Gordo began under the eye of General Scott, who had ridden out to witness it. Lee saw little of this assault. The column he was conducting had not gone far before it came under raking gunfire from the northern and western sides of Cerro Gordo. Part of the command had to be turned to the left to protect that flank. With the remainder Lee kept on. As he ploughed his way through the fire his thoughts turned homeward to Custis and he found himself wondering where he could have put the boy, to insure his safety, if the lad had been with him.16 Very soon General Shields was p245 ordered to swing around and take position to the west of Riley's division. With the left regiment scrambling along the sides of Cerro Gordo, the united force turned south to meet the troops that had swept over the crest.

Riley's troops had become somewhat scattered during the advance, and while they were being reformed for a charge on a five-gun battery on the Jalapa road, southwest of Cerro Gordo, Lee paused to help collect the Mexican wounded. Close to a little hut he came upon a Mexican boy, a drummer or a bugler, lying with a shattered arm under a dying soldier. Nearby was a little girl, probably from the hut, who was tormented by the plight of the boy, but unable to help him. "Her large black eyes were streaming with tears," Lee remembered, "her hands crossed over her breast; her hair in one long plait behind reached her waist, her shoulders and arms bare, and without stockings or shoes. Her plaintive tone of 'Mille gracias, Señor,'a as I had the dying man lifted of the boy and both carried to the hospital still lingers in my ear."[17]

Breaking his way toward Cerro Gordo through the chapparal, Lee mounted Creole and soon rejoined the infantrymen, who were now ready to attack the five-gun battery. They were met with only light fire as they dashed forward. A few minutes more, and the troops of Riley and Shields were across the Jalapa road, which was found as close to Cerro Gordo as Scott and Lee had expected it would be.[18] This turning movement can be seen at a glance from the sketch on the next page.

While this operation had been in progress, the attack on Cerro Gordo had been proceeding with equal success. The entire centre and left of the Mexican position was occupied, and the right of Santa Anna's army, near the river, was cut off from retreat, though General Pillow's attack along the Rio del Plan was a failure. The Mexicans on the right speedily surrendered, and Patterson's division in the centre, finding the pass clear, undertook to pursue the enemy up the Jalapa road. In this pursuit Twiggs's division and Shields's brigade also had a part. Before nightfall the remnants of the enemy were driven •ten miles and were broken into small detachments. Approximately 3000 troops p246 were captured, together with thousands of small arms and most of the Mexican artillery. Santa Anna himself barely escaped, on muleback, leaving his carriage, his headquarters equipment, his correspondence and his money chest to fall into the hands of the Americans. His forces, it subsequently developed, numbered about 8000, while Scott had 9000. The Mexican losses, which were never officially reported, must have run to hundreds. Those of the United States army, April 17-18, were 263 killed and 368 wounded.[19]

Lee came out of the action at Cerro Gordo, which was his first open engagement, with a new realization of the hideousness of war. He wrote Custis: "You have no idea what a horrible sight a field of battle is."[20] But if there could be glory for any individual in so much misery, it came to Lee from Cerro Gordo. He, a captain of engineers, had been one of the two officers to find the route on which the plan of battle had been based, and he had successfully led the turning-column on both days. His reasoning as to the position of the enemy and the location of the Jalapa road had been correct. He had disclosed a special aptitude for p247 reconnaissance, and by the possession of this quality he was commended anew to Scott, who leaned more and more heavily on him.

When the reports came in, Lee was mentioned in the warmest terms by each of the commanders under whom he had served. Colonel Riley said of him:

"Although not appropriately within the range of this report, yet coming under my immediate observation, I cannot refrain from bearing testimony to the intrepid coolness and gallantry exhibited by Captain Lee, United States engineers, when conducting the advance of my brigade under the heavy flank fire of the enemy."[21]

General Twiggs began a separate paragraph of his report to declare:

"Although whatever I may say may add little to the good reputation of Captain Lee, of the engineer corps, yet I may indulge in the pleasure of speaking of the invaluable services which he rendered me from the time I left the main road, until he conducted Colonel Riley's brigade to its position in rear of the enemy's strong work on the Jalapa road. I consulted him with confidence, and adopted his suggestions with entire assurance. His gallantry and good conduct on both days deserve the highest praise."22

General Scott mentioned Lee twice in the body of his report and outdid his lieutenants in this studied tribute:

"In expressing my indebtedness for able assistance to Lieutenant Colonel Hitchcock, acting inspector general, to Majors Smith and Trumbull, the respective chiefs of engineers and topographical engineers — to their assistants, Lieutenants Mason, Beauregard, Stevens, Tower, G. W. Smith, McClellan, engineers, and Lieutenants Derby and Hardcastle, topographical engineers — to Captain Allen, chief quartermaster, and Lieutenant Blair, chief commissary — and to Lieutenants Hagner and Laidley, ordnance — all actively employed — I am impelled to make special mention of the services of Captain R. E. Lee, engineers. This officer, greatly distinguished at the siege of Vera Cruz, was again indefatigable, p248 during these operations, in reconnaissance as daring as laborious, and of the utmost value. Nor was he less conspicuous in planting batteries, and in conducting columns to their stations under the heavy fire of the enemy."23

No other officer of the army received such high praise; none gained so much in prestige by the action. Captain Robert Anderson believed Lee to be the man best qualified by participation to write a history of the battle.[24] On August 24, though he did not get the news till much later, Lee was brevetted major, to date from April 18, 1847, "for gallant and meritorious conduct in the battle of Cerro Gordo."[25] Opportunity had come in his first battle; he had made the most of it.

---

**The Author's Notes: (Freeman)**

[1] Letter quoted (without date) in *Fitz Lee*, 37.

[2] *English Soldier*, 177; *Semmes*, 174.

[3] The honor of this initial reconnaissance is claimed both for Lieutenant W. T. H. Brooks and for Lieutenant P. G. T. Beauregard.

[4] The best map is in *Mexican Reports*, opposite p250. The ground is described in *Hitchcock*, 251-52, and in *Semmes*, 175. The clearest account is in 2 *Rives*, 395-98.

[5] Lee to Mrs. Lee, April 25, 1847; Jones, *L. and L.*, 51.

[6] Reconstructed from *Long*, 53, quoting John Fitzwalter; Jones, *L. and L.*, 51.

[7] *Cf.* 2 *J. H. Smith*, 50.

[8] *Hitchcock*, 250; 2 *Scott*, 432; Jones, *L. and L.*, *loc. cit.*

9 2 *Scott*, 445.

10 *Hitchcock*, 250.

11 G. O. No. 111, April 17, 1847; *Mexican Reports*, 258-59.

12 *Hitchcock*, 251.

13 *English Soldier*, 179.

14 *English Soldier*, 180.

15 Reports of Twiggs and his subordinates, *Mexican Reports*, 275 ff. For the placing of the heavy guns, see report of Colonel E. D. Baker, *ibid.*, 298.

16 Lee to Custis Lee, April 25, 1847; Jones, *L. and L.*, 53.

17 Lee to Custis Lee, April 25, 1847; *Fitz Lee*, 41.

18 Riley's report, *Mexican Reports*, 287 ff.; Report of Colonel E. D. Baker, who took command of Shields's Brigade when that officer was wounded, *ibid.*, 298-99.

19 2 *Rives*, 406.

<u>20</u> Lee to Custis Lee, April 25, 1847; Jones, *L. and L.*, 53; *cf.* to Mrs. Lee, *ibid.*, 51.

<u>21</u> *Mexican Reports*, 289.

<u>22</u> *Mexican Reports*, 277.

<u>23</u> *Mexican Reports*, 263.

<u>24</u> *An Artillery Officer in the Mexican War*, 191.

<u>25</u> *A. G. O.*, G. O. 47.

---

**Thayer's Note:**

<u>a</u> Lee's years of French studies at West Point peep through here. The Spanish word is mil; mille, pronounced the same way, is French.

Made in the USA
Monee, IL
07 July 2026

56550160R00023